WE ARE NOT ALL BLESSED WITH A HAT-SHAPED HEAD

To Keeley,
All the best,
Matt

ABOUT THE AUTHOR...

There are some people who have a distinctive voice. You wouldn't need to turn around at a party to check, if you were in a room with Ian Paisley! Or Alan Bennett. This is also true of poetry – there are some poets of whose work you only need to read a few lines to know who's speaking. When we say "voice" in terms of poetry, of course, we are not necessarily talking about a literal voice – though you only need hear a few seconds of that famous scratchy recording of Yeats reciting *The Lake Isle of Innisfree,* or Eliot reading *The Journey of the Magi,* for instance, to know who it is.

Almost always though, the voice we hear in our head when reading poetry is our own internal version of what we assume the poet must sound like. Many are lucky to have seen one of Matt Nicholson's performances and readings and therefore know what he sounds like in real life, but even if you had no idea of who he was, after reading two or three of his poems, the distinctive voice comes through loud and clear.

There is no mistaking a Matt Nicholson poem. As Goldsmith once said of Dr Johnson, "There is no arguing with him, for when his pistol misfires, he will knock you down with the butt!" Although this is not to say that it's all uncompromising tough-guy stuff. It was once said of another Hull poet, Andrew Marvell, that he had a tough reasonableness under a lyric grace, and that is something which equally applies to Matt Nicholson. Tough, yet reasonable. Dogmatic, yet understanding. You will also find moments of questioning, even of elegiac compassion, but it is always on his terms. His poetry speaks with an instantly recognizable tone, which echoes and resonates throughout his work.

There and back to see how far it is was the title of his first collection of his poems, which appeared in late 2016, in the *Humber Sound* series. That collection firmly established him as a poet with something to say. In this latest volume, *We Are Not All Blessed With A Hat-Shaped Head,* he has produced a cycle of work that will be warmly received by all existing aficionados of his work, those who have seen him perform at gigs, readings and festivals, and eagerly devoured by those who have come to his poems anew. Uncompromising, yes; tough, but oddly tender. Poems that will repay re-reading and which will stay with you, reverberating round your head in that unique Matt Nicholson voice.

Photo credit: Jerome Whittingham @photomoments

WE ARE NOT ALL BLESSED WITH A HAT-SHAPED HEAD

POEMS
by

MATT NICHOLSON

The Staring Owl

2018

ISBN 978-1-909548-81-7

WE ARE NOT ALL BLESSED WITH
A HAT-SHAPED HEAD
is typeset in
Book Antiqua and Gill Sans

The Staring Owl
is an imprint of
The King's England Press
111 Meltham Road
Lockwood
HUDDERSFIELD
West Riding of Yorkshire

© Matt Nicholson 2018

All rights reserved. No part of this publication may be reproduced, copied, stored in any retrieval system, or circulated in any manner whatsoever without the express prior written permission of the publisher. This book is sold subject to the condition that it shall not, by way of trade or otherwise, be lent, re-sold, hired out or otherwise circulated without the publisher's prior consent in any form of binding or cover other than that in which it is published and without a similar condition including this condition being imposed on the subsequent purchaser.

The author asserts his moral right to be recognised as such under the terms of the Berne Convention and the Copyright, Designs and Patents Act 1988 (as amended).

Printed and bound in the UK
by 4Edge Ltd
Hockley
Essex

**For those who know they don't know,
           and who care if they don't care.**

"Yes sir, a clown." he said. "There ain't one thing in this world I can do about folks except laugh, so I am gonna join the circus and laugh my head off."

Harper Lee – *To Kill a Mocking Bird*

Critical acclaim for Matt Nicholson's work.

We are not all blessed with a hat-shaped head is a poised, yet humble stride between moments of harshness and beauty, laced with vivid and tangible snapshots of everything in between. Nicholson's expert ability to bring those snapshots to life, on page and stage alike, has been well established over the years, but never more perfectly represented than in this collection. — **Geneviève L. Walsh**

From Lucifer sitting in a stolen yellow Lexus, to a blister on an allotment keeper's hand, this book will either make your stomach turn, or make the hairs on your neck stand up. More often than not it does both. It has that magical quality of being openly vulnerable, whilst also being laced with wry wit. Playfully sinister, morbidly uplifting, beautifully written - another stunning collection from one of my out-and-out favourite poets.
— **Matt Abbott**

Matt Nicholson's poems are a blend of the personal and the communal, the familiar and the curious. They disconcert, stroking your face gently with one hand and smacking you round the head with the other, but ultimately they steady and centre the reader with their reasoning. This collection is the life and the living.
— **Gill Lambert**

Nicholson's excellent second collection oscillates between moving personal poems of a quiet beauty and loud, visceral truths when he casts his perceptive eyes over society via our city streets and allotments. And through it all, we hear his big Hull heart beat on.
— **Mark Connors**

Contents

Prologue :

We are not all blessed with a hat-shaped head 13

Part 1: On the clock

Nostalgia and sin	17
Quantum sounds	18
Foreshore assumptions	19
An allotment of minutes	20
Wednesday's mood (a pathetic fallacy)	21
Scriptures	22
A lament	23
Don't shoot	24
Portrait	25
For the artists	26
Meditations after panic	27
This is a love poem	28
Mute	29
Translation into English	30

Part 2: Quarter past

Reluctant poet	33
Half-arsed-sonnet-type-thing	34
Schism	35
Outreach	36
Starling at the door	37
The bowhead songs	38
Air-raid warning	39
Apposite	40
Thug love	41
Augur	42
Ink-hand-dissent	43
My *Blackwing 602*	44
Silhouettes (in my peripheral vision)	45
Caress	46

Part 3: Half past

A memento from the sea	49
Horizontal light	50
Argument	51
221 Pershore Road – sometime in the early 90's	52
Low-sounding bells	53
Sliver	54
The opposite of entropy	56
The solipsism of one lost soul	57
The lingering look	58
Gone	59
Talking to no-one	60
January windows	62
Why we invent gods	63
When you realize	64

Part 4: Quarter to

Easter egg	67
Island diurnal	68
Alfresco	69
A priori	70
The blueprint for old friends	71
On the bias	72
Order of service	73
Down the hall (for Leonard Cohen)	74
We need to talk about…	75
Stalled	76
A simple war poem	77
America	78
Limbo	79
The end	80

Prologue:

We are not all blessed with a hat-shaped head

Sometimes,

when the only answer
is that life is just
a sensational series
of inconsequential moments
in oscillating orbit
around cold oblivion,

I sit up straight
and ask
a different kind of question,

maybe even
one about hats…

Part 1: *On the clock*

Nostalgia and sin

We would sometimes
play a game
with a full sheet
of postage stamps.

Taking turns
to tug
at a first class
stamp,

trying to tear
only one perforation.

And,
if we pulled
too hard,
and snapped
more than one
paper strand,

we had to write a note,
confessing
one proper sin.

And,
with the liberated stamp
stuck
to a brown-paper
envelope,

we had to post it
to a stranger.

Quantum Sounds

On *Wasserfall Straße*,
he is standing on the dry side.
He raises one eye
to the somnambulant sky,
like Bowie in Berlin;
in black and white,
in perfect light
on translucent skin.
As if he were born
for these scatter-gun clouds.

He is solving
equations of guilt,
balanced
by shorthanded penitence,
until that sweet, street song rises,
climbs its defended crescendo,
and unheard words
are just known;

the greater the heft
of the saxophone,
the deeper
the low notes sound…

The greater the heft
of the saxophone,
the deeper
the low notes sound…

Foreshore assumptions

If I stand here,

still enough,

quiet enough,

and frown,

dogs and walkers
assume I am
here to grieve,

that these frozen fingers
have tied *chrysanths,*
with raffia twine,

to some solid seat
beneath the swinging bridge.

An allotment of minutes

There is a man here,
working a walled garden.
Turning soil,
he makes decisions about the weeds,
about what is fit for compost
to grow better weeds next year.

He fights the kettle in his shed
and conjures unpotable tea,
as he remarks upon you and me,
under rusting, screw-thread breath,
that we are the wasters of days,
trespassing on his hours.

The blister on his spade hand
is at that point in its journey
where it might harden to a callous
or burst like an angry star.
Pausing, he spits into his ringing palm,
rubbing filthy hands together.

By noon, when the birds sleep,
he has forgotten about us, watching.
He is lost in a version of this world
that he governs as best he can.
Executing febrile plans,
he makes an ally of the rain.

And his day,
this old man working,
unlike ours,
the wasters watching,
will end up with an aching back
and a tale of unused time.

Wednesday's mood (a pathetic fallacy)

Wall at street end,

where words,

unspelled,

sprawl.

Where the young earn their titles.
Where hooligans fill out forms
and answer nature's call.

Grate above gutter
(leavings pass by and sink).
Echoes wilfully wander,
in untethered space,
as black
as complaint-letter ink.

Warmth is all but extinct
behind cracked corporation Perspex.
Where days demand a plan
but wet laces unwind.

And an empty hand
just forgets.

Scriptures

When we found him,
he was punching a bruise,
he was spinning on a broken toe,
and catching falling stars
between splintered fingers.

He was clawing at the air.
He was choking on the rain.
He was owning up to every crime
that was written on the walls.

When we found him again,
he was wearing our guilt,
he was staring at the sun
through migraine spinning eyes,
holding out his bleeding hands
to the travellers in time.

He was unable to move.
He was nailed to the floor.
He was singing with his eyes closed,
on his own and in the dark.

When we found him on a Sunday,
we saw right through him,
we knew that he was pain.
We knew that he was promises
made in the flash of regret,
that he was our salvation,
pledged, in the twist of an arm.

A lament

Talking to you
is like dropping rocks
into a galvanized steel bucket.

Talking to you
is like shaking a box full of rats,
hoping the fastenings hold.

Talking to you
is like sidling up to a moron,
whispering riddles into his ear.

Talking to you
is like walking past a gigolette,
on the other side of the street,
and feeling guilty
and relieved
at the exact same time.

Talking to you
is like finding the chromatography of blood
leached into an autumn evening sky.

Talking to you
is something that I do,
but still, I don't know why.

Don't shoot

I am a quiet man,
with deep voice,
and functioning delete key.

I have a large head
and broad chest,
and one medicated heart.

In simple silhouette,
against a blank-screen-glow,
I become a sniper's dream.

Portrait

When I see reflections,
on meniscus,
late at night,
I picture Sutherland's *Churchill*,
and my own first swats
at sugar-paper
with a square-ended,
water-coloured brush.
I hear Munch's *Scream*,
sedated,
as colours drown
in old glass jars.

For the artists

There is some kind of *splat*,
on canvass,
on a wall
in some gallery.

It boasts 48 colours,
allowing for the light.
I know,
because I counted them all,

and
wondered
how they overlap
like leaf-fall.

And there's a perfect square
of tooth-white card,
on the same wall,
beside this so-called *splat*,

explaining the artist's soul.

And I feel moved to ask,
in this modern world,

*who on earth
is going to read that?*

Meditations after panic

Brave gravity
pulls me back down to earth,
to a moment in time
when I know what I'm worth.

My heart is paper-wrapped
and placed on a table,
as I filter out my reasons
to feel lost and unstable.

And, while I remain focused
on breaking the sequence,
I embrace the value
of pure common sense.

Now I clear out the static
and the extraneous noise,
to re-find my beat
and my sense of poise.

And, in the silence
of this new conscious space,

I return to my sense of place.

This is a love poem

I wrote your name,
in chalk, on stone,
beside the black water pool
that reaches down into night,
and where light is extinguished
and all heat, neutralised.

And I drew a heart,
on stone, in chalk,
beside your name,
on the edge of that pool,
where water sinks to deepest black
and where night is manufactured
in the stolid stare of eternity.

And I wrote *forever*.

Mute

Your voice,
stripped back
to bones,
is modulated gas.

It must
be fracked
from deep
below the surface.

A voice,
once fracked,
will burn
till break of day.

Translation into English

It means,
come
and find me.

Or, it means,
please
don't lose me.

Or, it means,
I may be,
already,
lost.

Part 2: *Quarter past*

Reluctant poet

I am a reluctant voice,
sharing my words
like a kindergarten toddler
shares a toy
or his mother's holding hand.

I am a reluctant speaker,
spitting my words
like a prize-fighter
spits his blood
from his battered, beat-up mouth.

I am a reluctant writer,
scratching my words
like a lifer
scratches tally marks
onto a brick-built prison wall.

I am a reluctant dancer,
a reluctant friend,
a reluctant player
in this unthinkable script
and I long to be set adrift.

But, reluctant as I am,
I am all of these things…

except maybe not a dancer.

Half-arsed-sonnet-type-thing

She follows your scent across clammy nights,
carbon emissions lead her lonely chase.
She lands softly on your unbroken skin,
and finds that most irritating place.

Where your blood will pulse closest to the skin,
where a watch strap or a handcuff might chafe.
She waits until your mind falls fast asleep,
foolish and certain that your soul is safe.

And if she sticks you with her greed and hate,
those particles will reside in your blood.
She'll then move to her next naïve supply,
the same way that any parasite would.

Because she is your dark assasinette,
she is a dead-eyed sniper of the night.
And all that you will know when you awake,
is that tight and itching mosquito bite.

Schism

Let me tell you about Lucifer,
lost,
in a stolen, yellow Lexus,
somewhere
between Dresden and Prague.

The heat,
from continental, September sun,
is making the sweat run
across his red skin,
down the curve
of the small of his back,
to the curl
of his rudimentary tail.

And the radio jumps,
from Miley Cyrus to Wagner
and back again,
before it settles on the sound of a poet
reading over-written bilge
about the colour of a stolen car.

Outreach

Get thee to a library;
sit you down to read some fractured words,
or to a coffee-shop with books by the till,
full of thoughts rarely spoken, never heard.

Read one book, with a shot of something hot
from a flask or a corporate paper cup.
Wrap the chapters around your wind-blown legs,
unpick the definitions of *really down* and *up*.

And when the spine is lined from top to bottom,
and you have pushed those pages back together,
you need to search for that self-same writer,
you need to walk out in the afternoon weather.

And, when you find her (or even, maybe, him),
you need to cuddle up to that splintered soul.

Starling at the door

There is a starling
in the entrails bucket,
by the backdoor
of the butcher's shop.

He is fighting
the elasticity
of guts
and twisted sinew.

He is frustrated
by the constant interruption
of the butcher's
flying knives.

He is slick
with day-old blood,
but he keeps
coming back for more.

The Bowhead songs

Submerge your ears
beneath the surface sounds,
and listen
for the Bowhead songs…

*We are already old,
already old.
We are already old…*
they sing.

They have heard you
in the shallow water,
where your feet
disturb the sand.

They have seen you
tossed
on wounded waves,
where they, not you,
belong.

Now you must
dream your dreams
to the Bowhead's prayer,
to fathers boiled and gone.

As calves and mothers harmonise
their doleful incantations.

*We are already old,
already old.
We are already old…*
they sing.

Air-raid warning

He slips off the empty bones of ships,
part-down in the sand of the wave-wracked beach.
He is sure he can hear her voice, like a siren,
winding and waking a barbed-wire night.

And, through the half-open door, he sees her,
twisted around a stranger; mistletoe on an apple branch.
And the questions will come like air-raids
and leave their skyline scattered, a smoked-out horizon.

And though they may take
their bodies back to bed,
they will leave their shadows,
at war, on burning streets outside,
and they will live with the lies;
that women will forgive and will regret,
while men sleep so soundly
…carelessly forget.

Now that the chandeliers have fallen from this broken ceiling,
and search-light clouds shine through where there are no slates,
this feeling of falling off edges into boiling oceans,
ceases to be just a game.

Apposite

There has never been
a better time to try
pole-sitting in the rain.

To wring out wet socks
in milky puddles,
to scrape the leeches
off your brain.

To be the quiet edge
of a raging sea,
to sing surrender's
soft refrain.

But, when they ask of you,
the colour of your spine,
will you turn your back again?

Thug love

On your shopping list,
written with a crayon
clamped in your Neanderthal fist,
the words *RiCe cRisPies*
and *mELty cHocOlate,*
and in case you forgot,
you wrote it twice
and underlined it.

And I can imagine
your grip on that *Crayola,*
green like your tongue
and yellow like the sun,
hammering out letters,
lower case and capital,
and then, as if to go and cap it all,
you drew a heart above each *I,*
and I could almost hear you sigh,
like a real boy.

Augur

The ordinance of thunder
seems closer now.
The rain, falling
as heavy as
a solicitor's pen,
while we fix
all expectant senses
on the ancient
Bakelite phone.

Ink-hand-dissent

We write
because we have something to say.
We perform
to show that we do not run away.

We speak out
because we cannot comprehend.
We create
because we all decay in the end.

We react
because we are not yet dead.
We rage
because we have words not yet said.

We love
because that is all that there is.
We are bound together
against illusion and we must resist.

My Blackwing 602

Double-sharpened,
point and cone.

Cedar wood
and Japanese graphite

glide across this page
like an occluded front

rolling in
from the west.

A touch
too much indulgence?

A tool
of a lonely trade?

Maybe you are
a status symbol,

or just my costume
for this soul parade?

My *Blackwing 602*,
you are an enigma

and my friend.

Silhouettes (in my peripheral vision)

I do not cry
because I am brave.
I am on the tribulum,
wearing sandpaper shoes.
I am on the triangle point
of the sea-wall and falling.
I am evolved
into rubble and shards.

I am uncertain
and spared.
I am on the triangle point
of the sea-wall and falling.
I am on the tribulum,
wearing sandpaper shoes.
I am again
and against.

I do not cry
because I am brave.

Caress

My hand,
clasping your hand,
under simple covers.

This night,
so dark it forms a skin
to keep you warm.

Eyes closed,
in softest sleep,
you climb into the sky,

to look behind the stars,
for lost keys
to free the dawn,

for those permissions
that you need
to live beautifully.

Part 3: *Half past*

A memento from the sea

It was a pulling the pins from grenades moment,
a screaming into the void moment,
a telling you I was broken moment.

It was a red moment,
a dead moment,
an exploding sound in my head moment.

It was a spinning like tops
till the rain stops moment,
a counting the tears in your eyes moment.

It was a fried moment,
a tried moment,
a wishing I had lied moment.

Until you stopped for one great gaping moment,
and you tried to tell me that this tide was just a memory,
that these rocks, on this beach, had landed for one last time.

So, then, it took me just one more moment,
a that is that, goodbye moment,

before I picked a shell from the sand.

Horizontal light

There is a fire
in the furnace,
in the factory
of the sun.

Reservoirs
of relentless rain,
relent
and replenish.

Cloud machines
close down
for much needed
maintenance.

And a boy,
on a bicycle,
in the half-light
of this honest dawn,

pedals hard
towards
his own
horizon.

Argument

Instigation;

an experiment with the truth,
and we named gods
one after the other,
calling them after our injuries
until we ran dry of breath
and failings to pray for.

Post argument;

we stand,
propping up a sunset sky
on our zig zag bones.
Looking up through gravestone eyes,
until the stars burst through
and drown in dark water.

At your table, the next morning;

you fill in circles,
stay within pencil lines,
you add no colour to the foreground,
letting details fade to grey.

You have marked your face, with Indian ink,
and blotted the spread with softened skin.

221 Pershore Road – sometime in the early 90's

Waking, from those too fast,
ashtray-kissed nights,
to days that fizzed
too loud, like cherryade,
to days that were almost
and yet already done.

Sitting there, in sunshine,
on brick-burst, red-dust walls,
we swung legs
in cocky syncopation
with soft, imagined,
half-learned beats.

And today,
when our song broke into my chest,
staining ragged jeans once more
with lichen and brick-dust,
I made mosaic of shining memories
from old notebooks and glue,

for my half-remembered
you.

Low-sounding bells

Held down by the heft
of the low-sounding bells
that toll
on promising mornings.

The vacuum for the light
that illuminates hope,
the pulse in your neck
through your thin plastic skin.

I close curtains
to keep in your memory,
to stop you making more.

I cover your eyes
with off-cuts of carpet
where only we have walked before.

It was not perfect
at any point in time,
but it was yours
and it was mine.

Because there was
but now there isn't,
there might have been
but now there won't.

If I asked you to stay,
how far would you go,
on days that begin
with the toll
of low-sounding bells?

Sliver

We carry
our own-made models
of this world,
hung from our hairlines
and slung
between our ears.

And my eyes set out,
like armies, in flashes,
to capture new colours
and to confirm known edges,

to graze imagined skin,
or to scratch the itch
that sits, mocking,
on the end of my nose.

And I release hands and fingers,
like urchins into the fog,
picking pockets
and feeling for the facets
of hard and soft,

stealing heat
from matter
and from perfect form.

And, it is here,
where my thoughts grow,
like lichens,
that borrowed beliefs fizz
like over-the-counter remedies,
to create their own
self-contained sounds.

But hope lies,
when I send out my tongue,
like a beacon,
to land firm flavours
on suspicious rocks,

only to discover
that the map is wrong
and grapefruit
never went with chocolate
after all.

And we rely
on these made models
of this world.
And we live in them,
unrelenting and sure.

The opposite of entropy

Half-cut moon
hung, bent,
in mud-black sky.

Goose-winged clouds
scrummage
in shit-edged puddles.

Wind, like knives,
throws rain
down stone-dead streets.

And then I
hear you
laugh out loud,

and dive
into
the silence that follows.

The solipsism of one lost soul

Amongst the scratchings
left by broken mouldings,
I found him,
a hitch-hiker, ignored
by the passage of time.

He had been hiding
between dreams,
in those instances of idling,
in those solipsistic seconds
before the swallowing of sleep.

And, in this mirror's tarnished edges,
amongst harsh angles of the light,
we merged, for a moment,
me and him,
a solved equation
of all parts.

The lingering look

She moved aside the strands of fabric,
the satins, silks and lace,
the elastics and the stitching thread,
till she was gazing upon your face.
Because, she had painted, in her knicker drawer,
in oils, on plywood's grain,
the face you made when you said goodbye,
the face she would never see again.

Gone

I cannot say your name,
or write it,
with these fingers
in the steam
on this window,
because you have already gone.
And with you,
has gone my recollection
of the sounds
that name you,
has gone my knowing
of a world
that swallowed your light
and gathered
around your feet,
like disciples,
to hear you,
because you have already gone.
With you,
have gone the memories
that I cannot find or know to look for.
With you,
has gone the anticipation
of days
lost in time,
of days that will never be,
in this life
or any other,
because you have already gone.

Talking to no-one

i)
Right arm reaches two inches further
than the left, because of a break.
Rough pillow scars draw in three dimensions
on the right cheek, not the left.

And I pray to Jeezus that all is well with ya…
And your mammy had scars on her knees…
And they sent your daddy off to war
so you would have no kin…

ii)
She comes at dawn,
with water and cake,
and leaves it at his foot end.

She does not speak
or seek to be noticed.
She shuffles in her slippers
from a car left round the bend.

He is not fragrant today
but at least he's breathing.
There's a poor man's smile
in amongst his beard.

But she is gone
before the bin men start.

iii)

I'll not move unless you pay me.
He is trying his luck again.
The ambulance is waiting
and the gin is blotting out the pain.

I'll not move unless you make me,
and I'm a bigger man than you.
He's nursing a cut that will not shut,
and blood is filling up his shoe.

Ok, I'll move but you be careful now.
I could kill you all with just one breath.
And you'd better promise that you'll bring me back
if there is any of me that's left.

iv)

And I pray to Jeezus that all is well with ya…
And your mammy had scars on her knees…
And they sent your daddy off to war
so you would have no kin…
And I'll tell you now, what might have been,
if I had turned my back on sin…

And she waits for that resounding end,
when the breath has nowhere to go.
And she shuffles in her slippers
while she cries into her phone.

And she is there after he's been taken,
moving cardboard mâché to the skip.
And his words about her long-gone daddy
keep slipping from her lips.

January windows

There are frantic feathers
beneath a falling fog,
and cars puff steam
from tail-pipes.

Schoolboys swing bags
like turbo-props,
while girls make sense
of it all.

And the woman
at the window across,
of no specific age,
parts the blinds
with prehensile fingers,

keeping score
for a lonely god.

Why we invent gods

We long to live loved lives,
in the lowest levels
of the laziest sky.

Evolving far too easily,
on the ever-loving edge
of the eternity of space.

And we bend like biblical fishbones,
until we break like ostrich eggshells,
and there is nothing on the free man's face,
not even a speck of dust.

Because everything is falling,
flying without destination,
to a crash landing without warning
on the margins of all time.

We have to harness the hardest of hearts,
in the heaviest hours
of the haziest sky.

Un-answering unasked questions,
on the unrequited feelings
of a species, yet unresolved.

When you realise

It was in our eyes,
in the recoil of that Spring,
making promises written on blotting paper pages,
in the traction of the April rain.

It was in the garden,
at the end of that sated summer,
sinking heels into lazy lawns,
spilling wine onto uncut grass.

It was in the kitchen,
while leaves were jumping to their deaths,
that we made hot drinks in oversized mugs,
taking turns to turn the thermostat.

It was by the fireplace,
in the colourless corollary of Winter,
drinking whisky and eating chocolates
before climbing the stairs too soon.

Part 4: *Quarter to*

Easter egg

This shell is the colour of chapel-house tea-cups.

This shell is stronger because of the cracks.

This shell is shattered by repeated bird strike.

This shell is fractured by American bombs.

This shell is too small to house us all,
especially when you thrash like dying fish.

This shell, when viewed from out there in space,
is just a glass-eye set in a guide-dog's face.

This shell, made from plastic, and promise, and skin-cells.

This shell filled with ammonia, and fiction, and teeth.

Island diurnal

Daytime

Heliocentric hides,
stretched out,
scraped clean
of their television waste,
beneath the Calima's
soft-power,
skid-marked sky.

This air, so hot,
paint runs, like sweat,
down pure white walls,
and tarmac roads raise ripples,
become waves
that are ridden, by cars,
to the mirage.

Night

There is nothing there in the dark
that is not there in the daylight.
He is serenaded by the desperate song
of roaches,
until he sleeps with a hammer
tucked under his mattress.

He dreams, fitfully,
of making kindling from crosses,
and of something dark
and simply other.
And when he wakes,
wrapped in a salted sheen,
the sea is blue-bottle green.

Alfresco

I have no bones.

My arms are straight with bitterness.
My legs are stiff with hate.
My knee joints bend like rotted branches
in the teeth of awkward winds.

My ribs are made of promises,
too easily broken by a punch.
My toes are seedling acorns,
waiting for the snow.

I have no skin.

Fallen leaves and spider silk
clothe my frame to hold in screams.
The furs of feral beasts
wrap my menagerie of night.

I have no blessings,

no flesh.

I am devoured.

A priori

Come in,
out of the squall,
and tell me
that you are an angel.

Tell me
that you are a jester,
a bastard,
and a struggle.

Tell me
that you are not defined
by these repeated themes
that define you.

By these repeated fails
that betray you.

And then,
when the storm has passed,
you can scrabble about,
in the shifted sand,

for more of your
misshapen words.

The blueprint for old friends

You explained the workings
of spirals
and propellers.
You peeled the eyeballs
of wild cats
and snakes.
You walked the cliff-edge,
hands holding
grenades,
but nothing you could say
would make
me sway.

And we laughed, because
your ears
had grown.
And at your golden propensity
to shine,
even when
you played hide and seek
with the
village kids.

And we made pancakes and
sweet pastries,
until the
gas ran out, and the dirigibles
fell from
the sky.

On the bias

For all her skills;
her style,
her eyes,
her smile,
and the way
she held her hips;

she
        could
                not
        cut
                straight
with
        scissors.

Order of service

i)
This is the echo of a boy,
skimming stones across an ocean,
for eternal summer days,
to make a mountain at his feet.

He scales the steep elevation,
to reach the summit close to sunset,
to drink in its privileged view,
before he is called away
to dream.

ii)
I refuse to let go,
Blu-tack on cardboard corners.
I refuse to let go,
chewed gum in dirty hair.

I want to be better,
gods sanction more Tsunamis.
I want to be better,
a man gets eaten by a bear.

iii)
Each atom of the mountain
is another broken promise.
Each echo of the wind
is another crafted lie.
Each typed-out true confession
is the basis for a sermon.
Each poem penned in lemon juice
defines the angle of the sky.

Down the hall (for Leonard Cohen)

Eyes fail to focus,
limbs seek uncomfortable stillness.
Heart and lungs fight
over the scraps of his carcass.

He can hear the faintest,
tarnished saxophone,
caressed and whispered to,
just four doors past his own.

It's a strain to unpick this lover's tune,

but he can hear the sighs
of angels taking bets,
the grind of every line-drawn word
he used to shape regrets,
he can taste metallic spit and pleads,
Oh God, please, not quite yet!

With his heart
in one brown paper bag,
his lungs,
wheezing, in another,

he opens the apartment door
and, bouncing stiffly off alternate walls,
he moves on down the hall.

We need to talk about…

Some kind of intervention
would seem to be in order;
you are clearly out of order
and, so far, no-one has intervened.

All the lights were left glaring,
in that house we used to sleep in;
the doors were left wide open,
unanswered and unlocked.

They said that they had found you,
nose-deep in printed pages,
rocking back and forth quite slowly,
to the beat of saddening lines.

And I knew that they would find you
in that t-shirt that I gave you
to sleep in at the start,
before we were ground by time.

And yes, some kind of intervention
would seem to be quite timely;
you have fallen way beyond *untidy*,
and someone has to intervene.

Stalled (after 'The Mower' by Philip Larkin)

I read *The Mower*
through alcohol-slowed eyes,
on a wet Sunday morning,
divided.

I felt the time he described,
racing from the sky,
in the sheets of fast rain
outside.

We should be careful of each other.
But we do not seem to bother.

We should be kind while there is still time.
But we do not seem to be of the same mind.

Maybe the hedgehog was the lucky one.

A simple war poem

He is as splintered
as a bomb-blasted tree,
and bleached by dry air.

This man is just a casing,
leaking survival and heat
onto unfertilized earth.

His *oldman* was a bucket,
brimmed full of lessons,
with frustrations and blushes.

A life-time of trying
to shout louder than dogs,
than traffic, and clocks.

They shared one realisation,
it's about boxes and holes,
about fractions and wholes,

the knowledge that *destiny* and *fate*
do not give delivery dates.
They are just the machines
they cannot control.

America

There was blood on your cuff
as you pulled your jacket sleeve.
No-one saw it but me,
but now you're gone,
showered and changed,
re-arranging your face
for the world.

And the crowd are left
standing like threshed corn,
husked and red-neck raw.
Their eyes are fastened
to video screens,
sound-biting machines, that scream
until they're sore.

And three kinds protest;
the genuine, the entitled,
and those who must be seen
to be holding placards high
as cameras fill the sky,
and a dry wind
fills their lungs.

And we spin, where we stand,
like tops.

Limbo

Go,

take a walk
in a soldier's moment,

in the silence

between

flash

and

bang,

in the vacuum
that ties the ticking clock
to the fatal tock
without a maker's name.

The end

With coat hung up in the hallway,
and shoes well-worn by the door.

Notebooks dog-eared on the table,
and dreams spread out on the floor.

With skin washed clean in the bathroom,
and heart sleeping still in his bed.

There's a lesson he's learned on this journey,
one he's learned from the dead and well-read.

That a man
can only get close to the truth,
and we are not all blessed
with a hat-shaped head.

Acknowledgements:

I would like to thank my ever-patient wife, my parents and my brother, my extended family and friends, and all who have helped and supported in this endeavour, in particular: Pauline Massey (and family), Dave Mahoney, Carron Bailes, Karen Thorpe, Tim Allen, Gavin Burgess, Lisa and Gavin Khanna, The Protheroes, The Stringers, The Masons, The Glasspooles, Geneviève L. Walsh, Matt Abbott, Gill Lambert, Mark Connors, Joe Williams, Helen Shay, Joe Kriss, Gav Roberts, Vicky Foster, Richard Gammon, Joe Hakim, Dean Wilson and Jerome Whittingham.

With thanks to the following publications for publishing the following poems previously:

This is a love poem – algebraofowls.com Readers' Choice Winner August 2016

Sliver – visceralbusiness.wordpress.com October 2016

The opposite of entropy – Picaroon Poetry issue #9 July 2017

An allotment of minutes – atriumpoetry.com September 2017

221 Pershore Road – sometime in the early 90's – atriumpoetry.com October 2017

When you realise – Now Then Magazine February 2018